ANALYSING ANCIENT CIVILIZATIONS

THE ANCIENT Aztecs

Louise Spilsbury

raintree
a Capstone company — publishers for children

Raintree is an imprint of Capstone Global Library Limited, a company incorporated in England and Wales having its registered office at 264 Banbury Road, Oxford, OX2 7DY – Registered company number: 6695582

www.raintree.co.uk
myorders@raintree.co.uk

Text © Capstone Global Library Limited 2021
The moral rights of the proprietor have been asserted.

All rights reserved. No part of this publication may be reproduced in any form or by any means (including photocopying or storing it in any medium by electronic means and whether or not transiently or incidentally to some other use of this publication) without the written permission of the copyright owner, except in accordance with the provisions of the Copyright, Designs and Patents Act 1988 or under the terms of a licence issued by the Copyright Licensing Agency, Barnard's Inn, 86 Fetter Lane, London, EC4A 1EN (www.cla.co.uk). Applications for the copyright owner's written permission should be addressed to the publisher.

Produced for Raintree by Calcium Creative Ltd
Edited by Sarah Eason and Jennifer Sanderson
Designed by Paul Myerscough and Jessica Moone
Media research by Rachel Blount
Original illustrations © Capstone Global Library Limited 2020
Production by Tori Abraham
Originated by Capstone Global Library Ltd
Printed and bound in India

978 1 4747 9775 7 (hardback)
978 1 4747 9776 4 (paperback)

British Library Cataloguing in Publication Data
A full catalogue record for this book is available from the British Library.

Acknowledgements
We would like to thank the following for permission to reproduce photographs: Cover: Shutterstock: Yagujinskaja; Inside: Berkeley, University of California, 1903: p. 41; Flickr: Dennis Jarvis: p. 29; PX Here: p. 37; Shutterstock: BorisVetshev: pp. 1, 20; Ecco3d: p. 32; Gordon Galbraith: p. 11; Diego Grandi: p. 5; Dina Julayeva: p. 18; Schlyx: p. 19; Fedor Selivanov: p. 6; Studio Araminta: p. 15; Maria Uspenskaya: p. 38; Walters Art Museum: p. 39; Wikimedia Commons: pp. 4, 9, 14, 21, 27, 36; AndonicO: p. 7; Simon Burchell: p. 12; Daderot: p. 24; William de Leftwich Dodge: p. 43; Bernardino de Sahagún: p. 31; Emmanuel Eslava: p. 22; The Field Museum Library: p. 28; Geni: pp. 8, 45; Thomas Ledl: p. 42; Madman2001: p. 40; Joe Ravi: p. 23; Diego Rivera: p. 16; Diego Rivera/ Wolfgang Sauber: p. 35; Sailko: p. 25; Wolfgang Sauber: p. 17; Einsamer Schütze: p. 26; Jesuit Juan de Tovar: p. 33; Juan de Tovar: p. 10; Vassil: p. 34; Z-m-k: p. 13; Zuchinni one: p. 30.

Every effort has been made to contact copyright holders of material reproduced in this book. Any omissions will be rectified in subsequent printings if notice is given to the publisher.

All the internet addresses (URLs) given in this book were valid at the time of going to press. However, due to the dynamic nature of the internet, some addresses may have changed, or sites may have changed or ceased to exist since publication. While the author and publisher regret any inconvenience this may cause readers, no responsibility for any such changes can be accepted by either the author or the publisher.

CONTENTS

Chapter 1 The awesome Aztecs 4
   Aztec society 6
   Examining evidence 8
Chapter 2 Aztec beliefs 10
   Human sacrifices 12
   Life after death 14
Chapter 3 Secrets in stone 16
   Sites of sacrifice 18
   Doomed to destruction 20
Chapter 4 Work and trade 22
   Merchants and makers 24
   The codex painters 26
Chapter 5 War and warriors 28
   Weapons of war 30
   Prisoners and rewards 32
Chapter 6 Everyday life 34
   Family life 36
   Food and drink 38
   Entertainment 40
   The end of the Aztecs 42
Answers 44
Glossary 46
Find out more 47
Index 48

CHAPTER 1

The awesome Aztecs

The Aztecs ruled a vast **empire** in the area that is now central and southern Mexico during the 1400s and early 1500s. At its peak, the Aztec Empire spread over 207,200 kilometres (80,000 square miles) between the Pacific and Atlantic coasts of **Mesoamerica**.

Early Aztecs

The word Aztec comes from the name *Aztlán* meaning "White Land". Aztlán was the land in northern Mexico from which experts believe the Aztecs first came. The Aztecs believed that Huitzilopochtli, their god of the sun and war, told their people they should go in search of a new place to settle. They were told that they should build their new city where they saw a sign: an eagle devouring a snake while perched on a flowering cactus. The Aztecs roamed Mexico for about 200 years before they saw that sign at last on Lake Texcoco in the Valley of Mexico. To avoid conflict with the other tribes that were already there, the Aztecs settled in the swampy land by the lake in a city they called Tenochtitlan.

THE FIRST AZTEC RULER
Acamapichtli was the first ruler of the Aztecs of Tenochtitlan.

Expanding the empire

Tenochtitlan became a great **city-state** with a rich **society**. The Aztecs were a warrior people and every Aztec man was expected to train to fight. The Aztecs expanded the area they ruled outwards from Tenochtitlan, using their armies to take over new land. They formed an alliance with two other city-states: Texcoco and Tlacopan, fighting together against common enemies. Gradually, Tenochtitlan became the most powerful of the three and the Aztecs became leaders of a wide and great empire. By the reign of the last great Aztec **emperor**, Montezuma II, the Aztecs ruled over almost 6 million people.

RUINS OF TENOCHTITLAN
This is a serpent sculpture head on an Aztec temple in the ruins of Tenochtitlan, which is now Mexico City in Mexico.

Aztec society

The rulers or emperors of the Aztecs were the kings of Tenochtitlan, called Huey Tlatoani in the Aztec language. Aztec society was divided into different classes. The king was at the top of the social ladder and everyone else came below him in importance and status.

The nobles

Directly below the king were the nobles. The noble class consisted of government leaders, commanders, judges, high-level priests, landowners and lords. When an emperor died, a council of nobles chose the new emperor. The nobles had many privileges. For example, while ordinary people had to pay taxes to the emperor in the form of goods or labour, the nobles did not have to pay taxes. Nobles were also entitled to receive payments from ordinary people. Nobles got their status from their parents, and only nobles were permitted to display their wealth by wearing decorated capes and jewellery.

PROUD NOBLES
This sculpture was made by an Aztec craftsman and depicts a proud noble with an ornate headdress to show his status.

MASKED MEN
Masks were important in Aztec culture. The Aztec ruler, for example, dressed as the ancient fire god Xiuhtecuhtli when he became ruler.

The commoners

Commoners were the ordinary, working people. They lived together in communities owned by groups of families known as calpulli. Often, a nobleman and some older commoners led the calpulli. The commoner class consisted of farmers, artists, sculptors, doctors, **architects**, **merchants** and low-level priests. Artists and merchants enjoyed the greatest amount of wealth and respect within this class, and had their own **trade guilds**. The poorer people attended schools to learn their trades and to learn about religion, music and their language: Nahuatl.

Serfs and slaves

At the bottom of Aztec society were the serfs and slaves. Serfs did not own or share the owning of any land, and did not live in the calpulli. They worked land that the nobles owned. Slaves were criminals and prisoners, or people who were in debt and could not pay their taxes. Most slaves were prisoners taken in war. Slave owners were responsible for housing and feeding their slaves, and slaves generally could not be resold. Slaves were usually granted their freedom when their owner died.

Examining evidence

We can learn about how ancient people lived and who they were by examining pieces of evidence that they have left behind. We know a lot about the Aztecs by uncovering the remains of the many buildings they built.

Archaeologists at work

Archaeologists are people who find and dig up these remains. They can study the buildings to learn what tools and building materials the Aztecs used, what their cities were like and how different people lived. Temples tell them that the Aztecs were religious, and palaces tell them that the Aztec kings were rich and powerful. By digging under temples or following hidden passageways, archaeologists also uncovered **tombs** where rulers were buried with important **artefacts**, such as pots, weapons and other items that can tell us about past lives. We can also learn about the Aztecs from records made by the Spanish who invaded the country and took over Aztec lands in the 16th century.

SYMBOLS OF POWER
Archaeologists find pendants, like this one, which would have been worn across the chest by Aztec leaders. The doubled-headed serpents were symbols of power.

Picture records

The Aztecs also made books called codices. These contain pictures that reveal a lot about their lives. A codex shows scenes from everyday life and is an important record of the way the Aztecs lived. The codices show us that the Aztec emperor in Tenochtitlan did not rule other regions directly. The people were allowed to govern themselves as long as they regularly paid the emperors food and other goods, known as tributes. We know the extent of the empire because some of the tribute items, such as jaguar skins and exotic feathers, came from different regions. Tribute collectors lived in the conquered regions and made sure the payments were made and were on time.

ANALYSE THE ANCIENTS

This codex painting shows some of the tributes paid to Tenochtitlan. Based on the information you have learned, can you answer the questions to analyse the Aztecs? Check your conclusions against the Answers section on pages 45–46.

1. What did the regions that paid tributes to the emperor gain in exchange?

2. The painting includes items such as jaguar skins, not from Tenochtitlan, but from near the Pacific coast. What does this tell us?

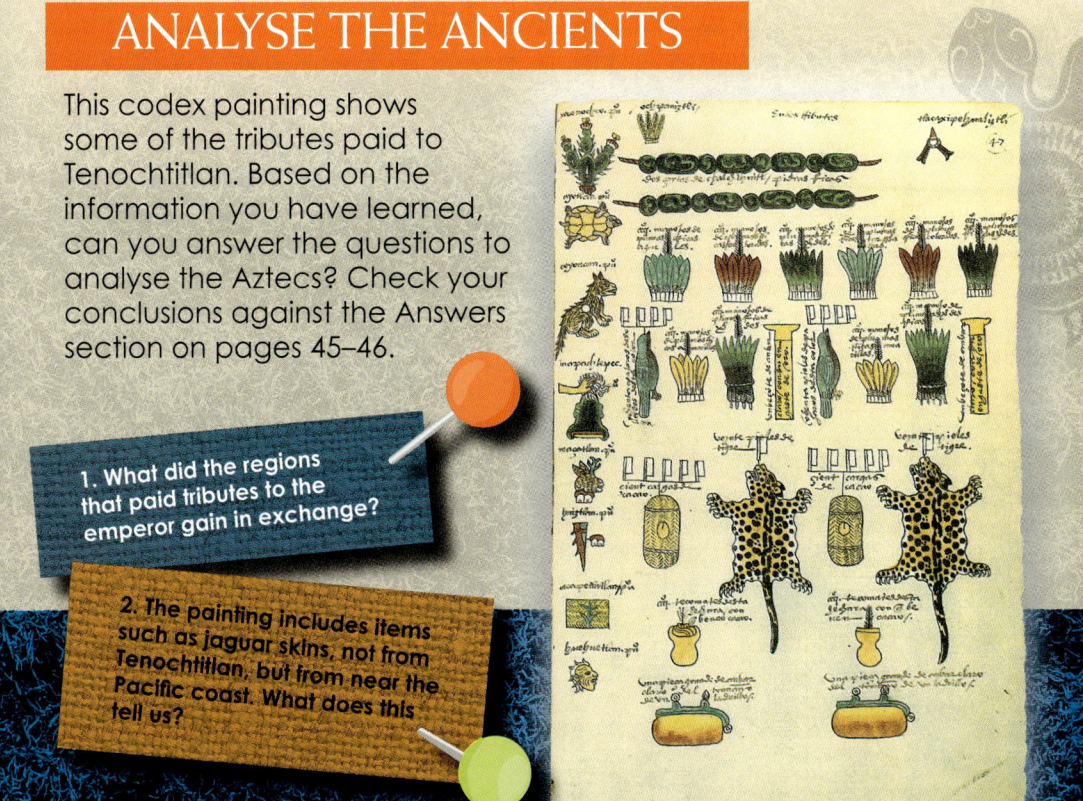

CHAPTER 2

Aztec beliefs

The Aztecs believed in and worshipped hundreds of gods and goddesses. One reason there were so many gods was that Aztec leaders were happy for the tribes they conquered to continue worshipping their own local gods, as long as they also worshipped Huitzilopochtli, the god of the sun and war and special guardian of Tenochtitlan.

The power of the gods

Each Aztec god ruled an aspect of nature or human characteristics. The Aztecs believed that the gods controlled everything in life. Each god had a good side and a bad side, and could make good or bad things happen to people. They believed that to keep the gods happy, they should give thanks to them. That is why the Aztecs built **monuments**, temples and statues for the gods and performed **sacrifices** as gifts to the gods. Priests made sure that the proper **offerings** and sacrifices were made. They also performed ceremonies in the temples to make sure the gods did not become angry and cause droughts, floods or other disasters.

THE MAIN GOD
This is an image of Huitzilopochtli, the Aztec god of sun and war. He was one of the most important Aztec gods.

GOD OF WIND AND WISDOM
This is a carving of Quetzalcoatl on an Aztec temple dedicated to the god.

Important gods

Tlaloc was the god of rain. If happy, he brought the rain that helped crops grow. If angered, he caused storms, thunder and lightning. He is often shown with fangs and large round eyes. To worship him, priests held ceremonies in which they bathed in the lake, mimicked the calls of water birds and shook fog rattles to call for rain.

Quetzalcoatl, whose name means "feathered serpent", was the god of wind and wisdom. Aztecs believed he invented calendars and books. As the god of learning, Quetzalcoatl was often worshipped in priest schools linked to temples.

Huitzilopochtli was the Aztec sun and war god, often represented as a hummingbird or an eagle. Aztecs believed he guided them to their home where they built Tenochtitlan. The Aztecs worshipped him by giving offerings of human sacrifices.

Human sacrifices

As part of their religious ceremonies, the Aztecs sacrificed thousands of people every year. The sacrifices took place in ceremonies on the flat tops of pyramid temples. Afterwards, the victims' heads were often displayed like trophies on a large rack.

Why human sacrifices?

The Aztecs believed that their gods sacrificed themselves to help the god who sacrificed himself to create the sun. They believed that to repay the gods for their sacrifices, and to keep the sun burning, they had to feed the sun god human blood and hearts. Without human sacrifices, they feared that the sun would stop glowing and without its warmth and light, everything would die. So to keep life going, the Aztecs regularly killed human victims in ceremonies led by priests. Those who were sacrificed were often slaves or prisoners of war.

SACRIFICIAL KNIFE
Ornate knives made from stone were used to kill victims of sacrifice. This knife is made from a stone called flint. The handle is in the shape of a crouching man covered with small pieces of mosaic stone.

Sacrifice ceremonies

Masks were an important part of all Aztec ceremonies, including sacrifices. Masks were offered to the gods in a temple or worn by priests and rulers for temple **rituals**. The most powerful masks were made of rare, costly materials, such as the precious blue stone turquoise. Turquoise was sacred, or holy, and represented life. In a sacrifice ceremony to the god Tezcatlipoca, a young man was chosen to live in luxury for a year, and spend his last week singing, feasting and dancing. Then he climbed to the top of the temple where the priests, wearing fearsome masks to represent the all-powerful god Tezcatlipoca, stretched him over a sacrificial stone and removed his heart.

ANALYSE THE ANCIENTS

This is a mask representing the god Tezcatlipoca. Using your knowledge of the Aztecs, can you answer these questions about the mask?

1. The mask is made from a mosaic of turquoise. Why was turquoise used to make the mask?

2. The mask looks especially frightening. Why do you think it was designed to look scary?

Life after death

The people who were sacrificed by Aztec priests felt honoured to be chosen. It was a great privilege to be sacrificed to the gods because the Aztecs believed this would secure them a place in paradise in the **afterlife**.

The Aztec afterlife

The Aztecs believed that people went to different places in the afterlife, depending not on how well they lived their life, but on how they died. People killed in sacrifice, or warriors who died in battle, went to a paradise that was the home of the sun. They helped the sun god rise each morning or fought beside Huitzilopochtli in battle. Women who died giving birth went to paradise and helped the sun god bring in the sun at the end of the day. People who died accidental or violent deaths, such as from lightning or drowning, went to Tlalocan, a paradise ruled by the god Tlaloc. Those who lived a long, healthy life and died of old age or illness, went to Mictlan, the Aztec **underworld**.

THE AZTEC UNDERWORLD
This image from the Aztec codices shows part of Mictlan.

DEATH MASKS FOR NOBLES
This death mask would probably have been placed over the face of a dead noble or royal to bring them back to life in the afterlife.

The Aztec underworld

In the underworld, a person had to travel on a dangerous journey, first by boat, then sinking down under Earth to finally reach the land of the Lord of the Dead. Once they arrived there, these people lived their afterlife serving the Lord of the Dead and living in darkness. Working for the gods in their afterlife was another way the ancient Aztecs tried to keep their gods happy.

Death masks

After an important or royal Aztec died, death masks made of precious materials were often placed over their faces. The Aztecs believed the death mask would bring them back to life in the afterlife. The masks were symbols that death was a continuation of life. Death masks were often made in the likeness of a god's face. Some were buried with a body or its ashes. Other death masks were offered to the gods or displayed in memory of the dead.

CHAPTER 3

Secrets in stone

The Aztecs were talented builders and craftsmen who made tools with chisels, hard stones and blades made from black volcanic glass called obsidian. They made a variety of great buildings and pyramids.

Tenochtitlan

The city of Tenochtitlan was built on an island in Lake Texcoco, which was enlarged by filling in surrounding marshy areas. The city was divided into four sections, called campans, and linked to the mainland by raised roads called causeways. The Aztecs also built a network of canals through the large city so people could travel around it by boat. The Aztecs built a double aqueduct (an artificial channel) that brought freshwater to the city because the lake water was salty. As the city expanded, the Aztecs had to deal with the sinking soil. To prevent the city from sinking, they used platforms as **foundations** or drove groups of tightly packed wooden piles into the soil. The Aztecs also built walls to protect the city from flooding, and freshwater **reservoirs** for people to use and to water farm crops.

THE CAPITAL CITY

Tenochtitlan was built around the public plaza, or square, at the centre, with temples and pyramids around it. Beyond the centre, there were homes, gardens and farming land. The city expanded until, at its peak, it had more than 200,000 residents.

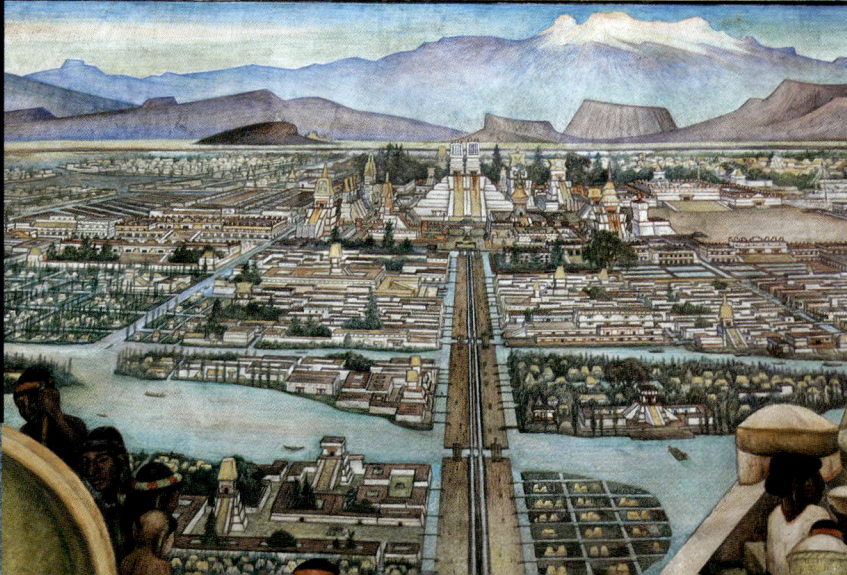

Palaces

There were many palaces throughout the Aztec empire. Some palaces were for the emperor to live in, others were in the countryside for him and his family to visit. Some had rooms where the emperor met with his officials to make laws and to plan for governing the empire. There were also halls where courts were held. The palaces usually had many rooms on two storeys surrounding a large courtyard. As well as living areas, there would have been libraries, storehouses, a reception area for entertaining guests and workshops for royal craftsmen.

Montezuma II's palace in Tenochtitlan had hanging gardens, a 10-room aviary filled with different birds and its own zoo with jaguars, eagles, pumas, foxes and snakes, as well as hundreds of other animals.

THE KING'S THRONE

This is Montezuma II's throne from his palace in Tenochtitlan. It is carved in the shape of a stepped pyramid and covered in carvings of Aztec symbols, gods and a picture of Montezuma II himself.

Sites of sacrifice

At the top of the unique Aztec pyramids, there were flat platforms for human sacrifices or temples used for prayers and other rituals. There was often a room that contained a sculpture or an image of the god to whom the temple was dedicated.

Types of pyramid

There were three main types of Aztec pyramids. The twin stair pyramid had a square-shaped base, two staircases and two temples at the top, each of which was dedicated to its own particular god. The second type of pyramid was less common: a round pyramid dedicated to the god of wind, Quetzalcoatl. The third type of pyramid had a square-shaped base like the twin stair pyramid, but it was smaller and had just one temple and one set of stairs. These pyramids were mainly found in smaller cities.

THE GREAT TEMPLE
The Great Temple of the Aztecs, in the centre of Tenochtitlan, had two temples on top, a wooden rack holding the skulls of sacrificial victims and many amazing sculptures.

The power of pyramids

The staircases of the Aztec temple pyramids usually faced west, where the sun set and descended into the underworld. Pyramids were often so steep and high that commoners at their base could barely see the temple on top. The temples were tall to show that the gods lived in the sky above the people and the Earth. Only those allowed to climb pyramids to the top, such as priests and rulers, could get close to them. At the end of the staircases there were often stone serpent heads, which looked like dragons. Aztecs believed the serpent heads warded off evil spirits.

ANALYSE THE ANCIENTS

These are the steps of an Aztec pyramid, leading to a high temple. Can you use the information you have read to answer these questions?

1. The steps have stone serpent heads, which look a little like dragons. What was the purpose of the heads?

2. The pyramid, with its temple at the top, towers over everything around it. Why did the Aztecs want the temple to be so high?

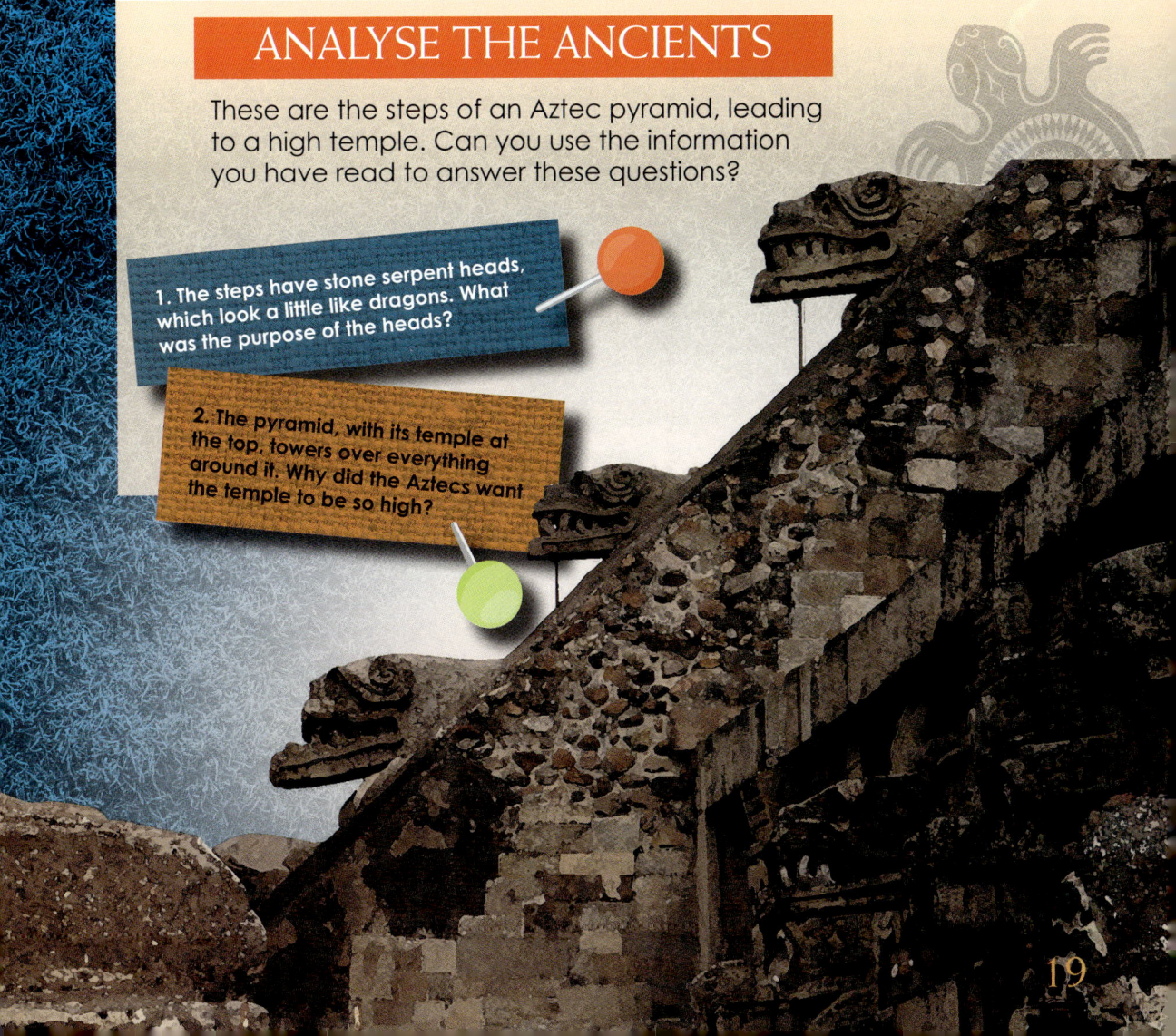

Doomed to destruction

The dates of many ceremonies held at pyramid temples were marked by calendars carved in stone. The Aztec calendar had a sun calendar to measure time, with a ritual calendar for religious festivals. The calendar also foretold the end of the world.

The Sun Stone

At the centre of the Sun Stone calendar is the face of the sun god. It represents the Aztec belief that the universe had passed through four world creations, which had all been destroyed. The Aztecs believed that they lived in the fifth creation, and that they were doomed to be destroyed by a huge earthquake. The sun god in the middle holds a human heart in each hand, his outstretched tongue represents a ritual knife. This was a symbol of the Aztec belief that human sacrifice ensured the continuation of the sun, and all life.

MEASURING TIME
The Sun Stone calendar is the largest Aztec sculpture ever found, measuring 4 metres (13 feet) in diameter and weighing about 25,000 kilograms (25 tonnes).

BINDING OF THE YEARS
This codex image shows the gods Tlaloc and Huitzilopochtli in their temple. It also shows the skulls of the people the Aztecs sacrificed to these gods in religious ceremonies, which were scheduled according to the sun calendar.

How does it work?

The Sun Stone is sometimes called the calendar stone because it shows two calendar systems, which are different but linked:

- The 365-day xiuhpohualli calendar describes the days and rituals related to the seasons. It contains 18 months of 20 days each, plus five unlucky days when the Aztecs believed disasters might happen. Around the central image of the sun god, there is a band of 20 different day symbols.
- The 260-day tonalpohualli calendar divides the days and rituals between the gods. Every 24-hour cycle has 1 of 20 day names (such as jaguar or wind) and a number from 1 to 13, because Aztec weeks lasted 13 days.

The Sun Stone calendar worked a little like two linked wheels. By linking the date on one wheel to the other, no date could be repeated for 52 years. The Aztecs believed that when that day came, the universe was in great danger. So every 52 years, they performed a ceremony called the Binding of the Years to prevent disaster.

CHAPTER 4
Work and trade

The Aztecs had a wide range of jobs and made goods that they were able to trade with peoples far away. Farming was a very important part of Aztec life and a reason for its early success. Using smart farming techniques, the Aztecs were able to build up islands on the swampy land of the lake where they could grow crops. This allowed them to grow more plants than any other farmers in the world at that time, and this success allowed them to feed a growing population.

Floating farms

The Aztecs grew their main crops on several little islands that they constructed on swampy shallow lake beds. These were called chinampas. They were made by building up thick layers of plants taken from the lake surface, mixed with mud from the bottom of the lake. The Aztecs planted trees and placed stones around the edges of the chinampas to make them stable. They left strips of water, like canals, between them so they could reach their plots by canoe. Aztec farmers had no ploughs and they did not use animals to help them farm. They relied on hard work and simple tools, such as stone hoes on a wooden stick used to turn the dirt, and a type of shovel with a long handle and a flat stone head.

TRAJINERAS
The Aztecs used flat boats called trajineras to travel among the chinampas, where they grew food crops.

Markets

There were markets all over the Aztec lands, where farmers and other producers could bring their food and other goods to sell. In Tenochtitlan, there were markets throughout the city and a main marketplace where up to 40,000 people could gather to buy and sell goods and food. Officials carefully controlled the prices at the markets, and there were always officials on hand to stop arguments or arrest anyone who tried to steal goods. Some people **bartered** for goods, and some goods functioned as money, including cacao beans, small squares of cotton cloth, small gold nuggets, pieces of tin and rare feathers.

AZTEC MARKETS
This model shows a bustling market at the Aztec city of Tlatelolco.

Merchants and makers

The Aztecs made a variety of useful and decorative objects for themselves, the temples and to sell at city markets or for merchants to trade with other cities.

Merchants on the move

The Aztec merchants, known as pochteca, travelled vast distances on foot to buy and sell objects. They **exported** luxury items such as jewellery, as well as lake salt and pottery. They **imported** items such as jewellery, textiles, animal skins, rare birds and their feathers, rubber and a precious stone called jade. They traded goods from as far away as what is now southern New Mexico, USA. Raw materials from Central America arrived in the markets of Tenochtitlan. Merchants were extremely important and could pass their job and land down to their children.

Craftspeople at work

Aztec potters made simple pots for use in the home and more ornate pottery for rituals. Some craftspeople were skilled at using colourful feathers to make fabulous garments and headdresses for the nobles and royals.

SKILLED POTTERS
The Aztecs usually painted decorations on their pottery in two colours. Here black and red are used on an orange ceramic plate.

Golden objects

The Aztecs believed that gold was the sun's **faeces** and was therefore sacred, so goldsmiths had a high status among craftspeople. Gold objects, such as labrets, were worn only by high chiefs and royalty. Labrets were a type of plug worn below the lower lip to symbolize the fact that the ruler spoke for the gods. Some labrets were shaped like serpents, creatures that slither on the ground, in water and among forest trees, just as a god might move on land, in water and through the sky. These serpent-shaped labrets had a tongue that could move. Labrets would have been worn on ritual occasions and on the battlefield, to strike awe and fear into the hearts of those who saw them.

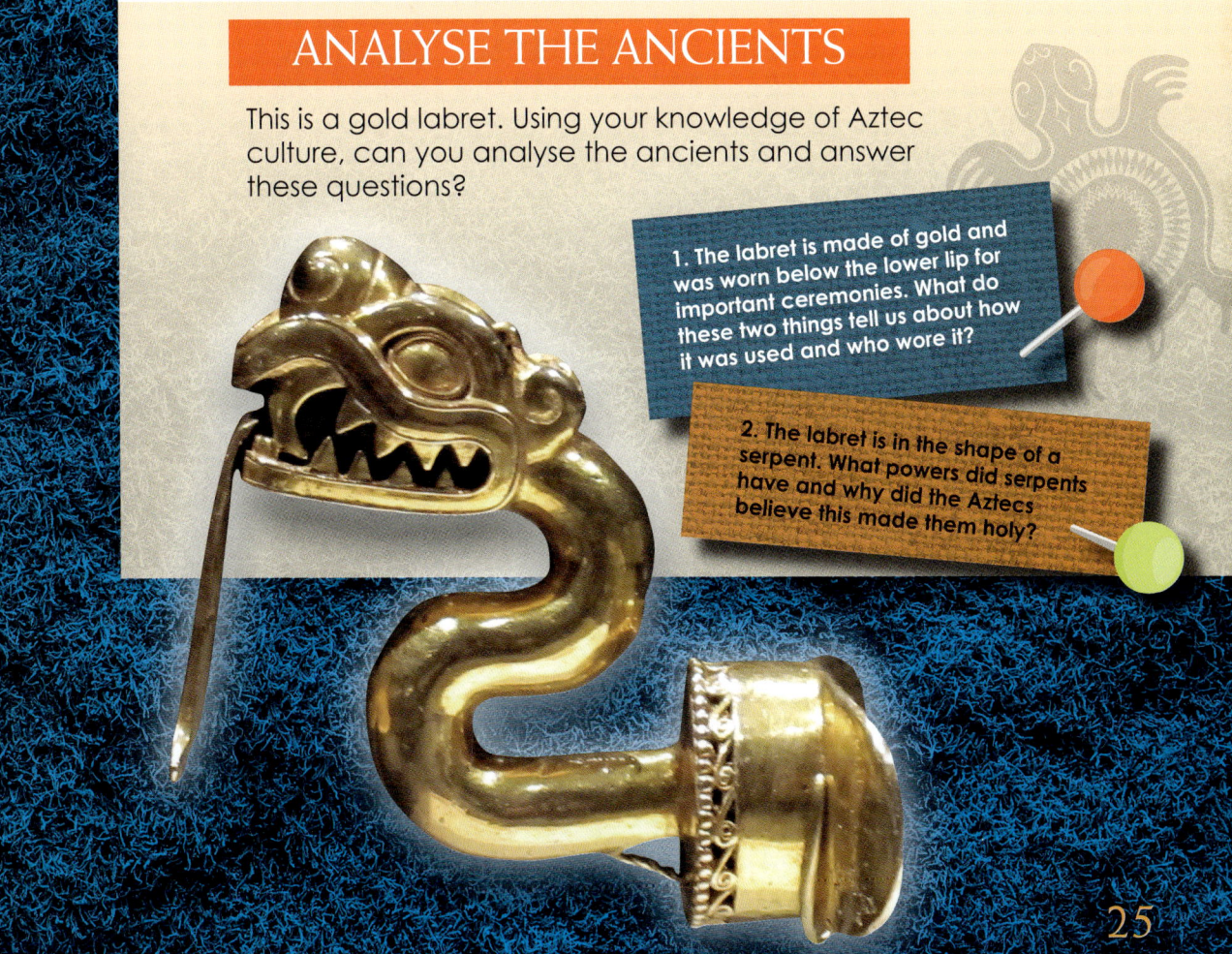

ANALYSE THE ANCIENTS

This is a gold labret. Using your knowledge of Aztec culture, can you analyse the ancients and answer these questions?

1. The labret is made of gold and was worn below the lower lip for important ceremonies. What do these two things tell us about how it was used and who wore it?

2. The labret is in the shape of a serpent. What powers did serpents have and why did the Aztecs believe this made them holy?

The codex painters

Merchants needed people to keep records of all their trades and profits. In fact, a lot of paperwork was required to keep the large Aztec Empire running smoothly. Records were kept of many things: the events of the Aztec year, taxes and tributes, temple rituals, lists of who belonged to the ruling class, laws and court cases, property and ownership lists. The codex painters carried out all of this official work.

Codex pictograms

Being a codex painter was an important job. Most codex painters were nobles who were trained in the calmecacs, which were the advanced schools of the noble class. They had to learn all of the different pictograms the Aztecs used. Pictograms are little pictures that represent different objects. The codex painters had to learn the pictograms and symbols or pictures that represented an idea too. For example, the idea of death was represented by a picture of a dead body wrapped for burial; night was represented by a black sky and a closed eye; and walking was represented by a trail of footprints.

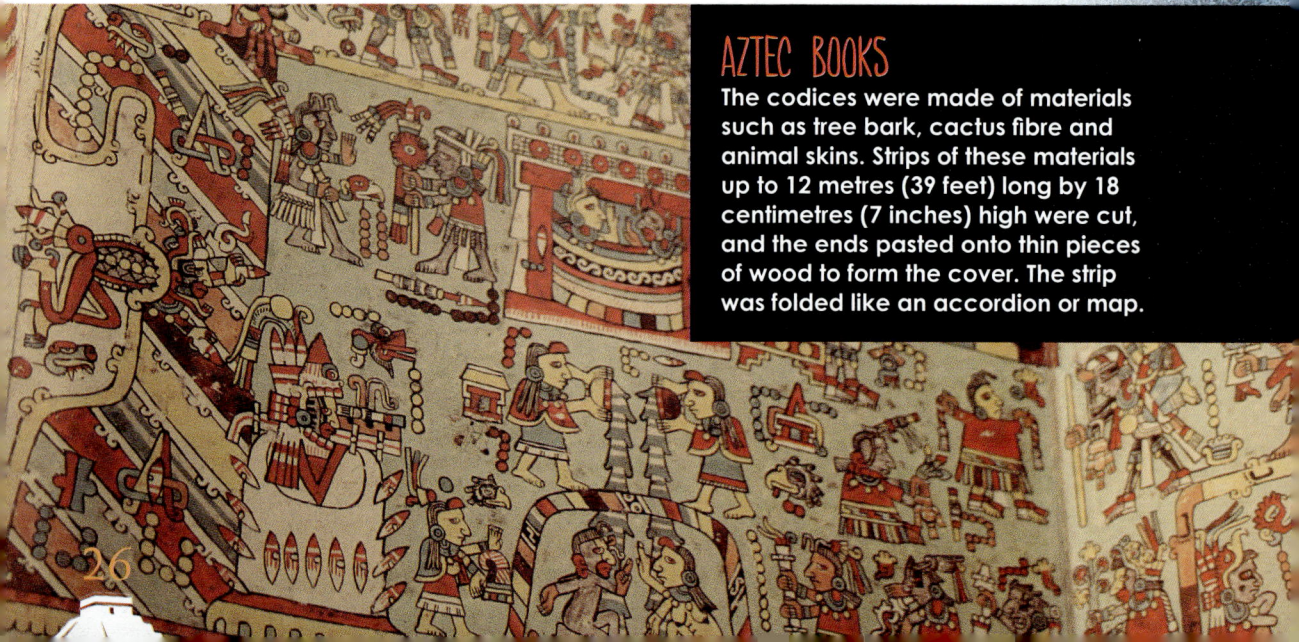

AZTEC BOOKS
The codices were made of materials such as tree bark, cactus fibre and animal skins. Strips of these materials up to 12 metres (39 feet) long by 18 centimetres (7 inches) high were cut, and the ends pasted onto thin pieces of wood to form the cover. The strip was folded like an accordion or map.

DAYS OF THE MONTH
This is a page from the Codex Borgia, one of the most beautiful surviving Aztec codices. Many of the pictograms in this codex represent days of the month in the Aztec calendar.

Counting on the codices

The codex painters also had to learn how to illustrate numbers and how to count. The Aztec number system was based on 20, probably because people have a total of 20 fingers and toes. Numbers 1 to 19 were represented by dots. A little flag or banner represented the number 20, and five bags or banners represented 100. A picture of a feather meant 400, and a bag or pouch of **incense** represented 8,000. The Aztecs used these symbols to count and record all their tributes and trade. For example, a tribute page showing 18 dots, 5 flags and 1 pictogram of a shield meant that 118 shields had been sent to the emperor.

CHAPTER 5

War and warriors

The Aztec Empire was created and controlled by the force and might of its warriors. The Aztec armies conquered new regions and tribes of people, then helped keep them under control, so the empire could expand and remain powerful.

Aztec armies

All Aztec men, even the priests, were trained to fight and were expected to take part in battles, at least when they were young. The king was the commander-in-chief of the armed forces. He had a second-in-command and a war council of high-ranking nobles, who planned battles and controlled different units of warriors. The Aztecs did not have a permanent army as such. Instead, each town was expected to supply up to 400 warriors when needed. Each of these units might be led by one of their own high-ranking warriors or become part of a larger unit of 8,000 men. For major battles, there could be up to 25 units of 8,000 men, totalling 200,000 warriors in all.

AZTEC WARRIORS IN COSTUME
These are Aztec warriors as pictured by a codex painter. The higher the rank, the more elaborate a warrior's costume.

Symbols of rank

Aztec warriors had different symbols of rank to show how important they were in the army. Some wore ornaments such as lip, nose and ear plugs. High-ranking Aztec warriors wore feathered capes or suits. If they also wore a feathered headdress that towered above their shoulders, they were high-ranking officers. The best warriors were named jaguar or eagle warriors. Eagle warriors wore helmets with open bird beaks, a costume with eagle wings, and even imitation talons (bird claws) on their legs. The deadliest Aztec warriors were named "the shaved ones". These warriors had one long braid on the left side of their heads and the rest was shaved.

EAGLE WARRIORS

This is a life-size sculpture of an Aztec eagle warrior. It once stood next to the Great Temple of the Aztecs in Tenochtitlan. The eagle was the symbol of the sun god, to whom all sacrifices were offered. So the eagle warriors were among the most important of all.

Weapons of war

Older Aztec warriors trained younger warriors in military tactics and how to use weapons and win battles. Later, young men followed armies into battle, carrying bags and supplies so they could watch and learn from the older warriors. When they finally captured their first prisoner, they were considered warriors. They could then cut off the long braid that had been growing since they were 10 years old.

A warrior's weapons

The trainee warriors had to learn to use a variety of weapons. These were made of wood and stone, but never metal. Some were for fighting at close range and others were for longer distance combat. The macuahuitl was a wooden club that had a row of razor-sharp obsidian blades sticking out from the edge. Obsidian could be cut to have dangerously sharp edges, making the macuahuitl a deadly weapon. They also carried spears made from wood that had a blade with an obsidian edge. All Aztec warriors carried a round shield for protection. Some shields were made from jaguar skin and feathers from turkeys, ducks or colourful tropical birds.

DEADLY MACUAHUITL
This is a modern reconstruction of an Aztec ceremonial macuahuitl.

DECORATING A SHIELD
This Aztec painting shows a feather artist creating the outer feather layer for a warrior's shield.

Long-range weapons

Aztec bows and arrows had a sling made from cactus fibre thread, and an arrow made from wood with a sharpened end. An atlatl was a long stick with a grip at one end and a hook to grip the spear at the other. This weapon allowed a warrior to throw a light spear much further and faster than by hand alone. It had first been used for hunting but could hit an enemy from around 150 metres (500 feet) away! Although these weapons were dangerous, the main aim of the Aztec warriors was to capture most of the people they attacked rather than kill them. A warrior who killed instead of captured too many enemies lost respect.

Prisoners and rewards

Aztec warriors believed that the wars they fought were sacred. They believed that they needed to capture people who could be used as human sacrifices in the temples on top of the pyramids. That would keep the sun moving across the sky and give life to people on Earth.

Rich rewards

If you were an Aztec commoner, the only way to leave the lower classes and move up in the world was to become a successful warrior. The more prisoners that warriors captured and the braver they fought, the more rewards they would receive. They were rewarded with expensive gifts and honoured and praised in public. If they reached the rank of eagle or jaguar warrior, they became nobles. As farmers, they had a share of land they farmed. As successful warriors, they were given shares of other lands that they conquered, which other people worked for them. They could become army leaders and commanders. When not at war, they worked to police the cities and protect merchants on long trips.

PRISONERS OF WAR
Prisoners captured in war were used as human sacrifices. Their skulls were stacked up outside on racks, represented here by carvings on the stone wall of a temple.

Jaguar warriors

Aztec warriors who captured a lot of prisoners were rewarded with magnificent eagle or jaguar costumes. The more prisoners they captured, the more elaborate their costumes became to show how successful and brave they were. Jaguar warriors covered their bodies in jaguar skins. The Aztecs regarded the jaguar as the bravest of beasts and the jaguar represented Tezcatlipoca, god of the night sky. Aztecs also wore jaguar costumes at war because they believed the skins gave them the strength of jaguars during battles. Jaguar warriors often led other warriors into battle so that the enemy, who also thought of jaguars as mighty killers and identified them with magic, would be terrified.

ANALYSE THE ANCIENTS

This codex image shows two warriors in jaguar costumes. Using information you have read about Aztec warriors, can you answer these questions?

1. The jaguar costume was probably the actual skin of a jaguar. What did the jaguar skin mean to the Aztec warrior wearing it and to the enemies he attacked?

2. What is this jaguar warrior holding in his left and right hands? What were they likely to have been made from?

CHAPTER 6

Everyday life

The houses the Aztecs lived in, the food they ate and the clothes they wore all differed depending on the class to which they belonged.

Houses and homes

Nobles usually lived in large two-storey houses made of stone and sundried bricks. The houses had flat roofs, some with a garden on top, and were built around a central courtyard. There were separate living rooms, bedrooms and kitchens, as well as rooms where servants and slaves lived. Rich people also took a cleansing steam bath every day, in a building where water was poured over hot stones to create steam.

Commoners' houses were much simpler and were often more like huts made of reeds plastered in clay. They often had only one main room and very little furniture. Women and girls wove mats from reeds for the floor. The family slept on thicker versions of these mats. Each home had a garden where the family grew food for itself.

AZTEC MIRRORS
Women began the day by washing and looking into obsidian mirrors, like this one. The women tied up their hair and sometimes wore red paint around their mouths.

REIMAGINING THE PAST
This is a wall painting by a 20th-century artist named Diego Rivera. It shows the outfits worn by traders in an ancient Aztec market.

Clothes and accessories

Slaves would wear only a simple loincloth – a long strip of cloth wrapped to form a short skirt and tied in front. Men also wore triangular cloaks or ponchos over their shoulders. Women wore a shirt with a skirt wrapped around their hips. These garments were usually made of cotton and undecorated. If people were a little wealthier, their garments might have **embroidered** or fringed ends. People of high rank wore elaborate costumes, which were colourfully embroidered and often decorated with feathers. Feathers were a clear sign of status. Jewellery such as necklaces, earrings and bracelets were also worn by the upper classes. Most of the Aztecs walked barefoot everywhere. Only the upper classes and warriors wore sandals.

Family life

The kind of life you lived in an Aztec family depended on whether you were a girl or a boy. This is because the Aztecs had quite different expectations of what men and women would do with their lives.

Birth rituals

When a baby was born, the kind of ritual carried out to mark the occasion was different for boys and girls. For boys, a new shield was placed in his left hand and a newly made arrow was placed in his right hand. Then, a successful warrior buried the baby's **umbilical cord**, along with the shield and arrow, beneath a battlefield. The Aztecs believed these ceremonies would help the boy become a good warrior when he grew up, and show how important warriors were to their survival. If the baby was a girl, the family buried her umbilical cord under the family fireplace. This symbolized that her future was in the home, taking care of her family and working in the household.

FAMILY TREES

Family was important to the ancient Aztecs. One family had their family tree made from clay.

DOLLS AND TOYS
Experts think Aztec children might have played with toys, like this doll made from clay.

Growing up

Most Aztec boys grew up to be farmers and tradesmen, learning the skills of their job from their fathers. Girls learned household skills from their mothers. Education was important to the Aztecs so children also went to school. The Aztecs were one of the first societies to provide free schooling for all children. However, rich and poor children, boys and girls, as well as slaves, all went to different schools.

Schools were often linked to a temple, so children were taught about their religion and the rules they had to follow. They were also taught the songs and dances that were part of religious ceremonies. Boys also received training to teach them to be good warriors. If a child was particularly good at a subject, such as maths, they would be moved into a special class for that subject. The Aztecs knew that it was important to make the most of people's talents.

Food and drink

The Aztecs ate what they could grow and hunt. This was because they did not raise farm animals. It was easier to grow crops than to catch wild animals so the Aztecs mainly ate vegetables and grains.

Daily foods

Rich people ate some meat, such as turkey or wild dog. However, meat was in short supply, so poor people seldom ate it. Poor people did however sometimes eat insects and insect eggs. The Aztecs ground up maize on a grinding stone to make it into flour. They rolled it flat to make tortillas. They also ate corn on the cob and used the corn kernels in soup. They shaped dough into balls, stuffed it with beans and vegetables, and wrapped the balls in maize leaves or husks to make tamales. Beans were soaked in water, cooked until soft, then added to soups and stews. They also ate a wide range of vegetables and fruits, including chilli peppers, sweet potatoes, tomatoes, onions, avocados, aubergines, pumpkins, papayas and pineapples. As well as eating the pineapples, they sometimes hung their spiky tops outside the hut door as a sign that friends were welcome to drop in.

PRICKLY TREATS
The Aztecs also ate the fruit of the prickly pear cactus, which they called nopal.

TRIPOD POTS
Aztec nobles liked their food to be served in this style of shiny, painted pots. This is a tripod pot, with three legs.

Feasts and treats

The Aztecs ate some foods that are similar to treats people eat today. They used cacao beans to make a kind of hot chocolate, flavoured with vanilla. This was the nobles' favourite drink. They crushed peanuts into a thick brown paste, much like the peanut butter people eat today. They also combined cracked nuts with boiled honey to make a kind of peanut brittle sweet. They even had chewing gum in the form of chicle, a **resin** extracted from the sapodilla tree. The Aztecs realized that it was also useful as a breath freshener.

Entertainment

The Aztecs worked hard, and warriors were often in danger, but they also knew how to enjoy themselves. They entertained themselves with music, song, dance and games. Sports were so popular that the best athletes became celebrities.

Music, song and dance

Like so much of Aztec culture, music, song and dance were closely linked with religion. They were an important part of feasts and ritual ceremonies and celebrations. There were no string instruments, but there were whistles, rattles, trumpets, flutes and drums. Drums were often made from hollow logs and some were made from turtle shells. Rattles were made from dried gourds, which are large, hard-skinned fruits.

AZTEC DRUMS
Aztec drums were designed to be played horizontally, like this one, or vertically.

Board games and sports

Patolli was a board game in which players had to move a set of pebbles from one end of a mat or board to the other end. The mat was divided into four parts with safe and penalty squares. Moves depended on the throws of five beans, which were marked on one side and plain on the other, similar to today's dice. It was a gambling game, and people bet whatever they could afford: blankets, plants, precious stones, gold, food and – in extreme cases – their homes or freedom. Even games had a religious side to them, with players offering prayers to Xochipilli, the god of games, to help them win.

Nobles, high-ranked warriors and some professional players played ball games on large stone courts. In one game, teams battled to be first to move a heavy, solid-rubber ball through a stone hoop high up on a wall. Ball games were linked to the religious idea of a daily fight between the sun and the darkness, or life and death, and people often gambled on the results.

ANALYSE THE ANCIENTS

This codex image depicts Aztecs playing patolli, being watched by Xochipilli, the god of games. Can you answer these questions using your knowledge of the Aztecs?

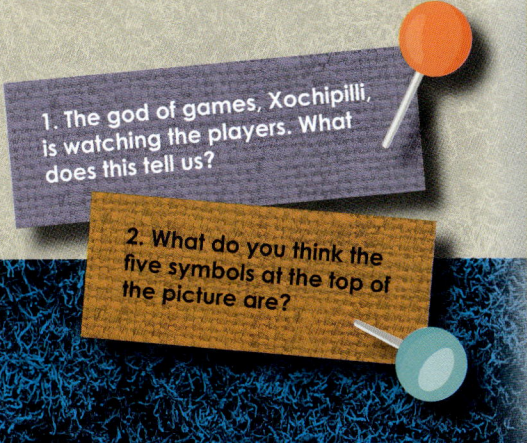

1. The god of games, Xochipilli, is watching the players. What does this tell us?

2. What do you think the five symbols at the top of the picture are?

Fig. 18. *Juego de patolli (Códice Magliabecchi)*

The end of the Aztecs

The Aztecs were one of the world's greatest **civilizations**. Their civilization came to an end after the Spanish invader Hernán Cortés sailed from Europe to what is now Mexico and conquered the once-great empire.

Spanish invaders

Montezuma II was the Aztec Empire's last ruler and his reign lasted for 18 years. During that time, Aztec warriors continued to expand the empire, but conquered peoples were becoming increasingly annoyed about paying tributes. When the Spanish arrived in 1519, Montezuma II first welcomed Hernán Cortés and gave him gifts of gold. However, Cortés was not to be trusted. He promised the disgruntled American Indians that they would be freed from paying tributes if they helped him overthrow Montezuma II. With their help, Cortés and his men, who wore steel armour and carried metal weapons, were able to attack and ultimately defeat Montezuma II and take over the city of Tenochtitlan.

FEATHERED HEADDRESS
This is a feather crown that belonged to the Aztec emperor Montezuma II.

LAST DAYS OF TENOCHTITLAN
This is a 19th-century painting depicting the final battle during the Spanish invasion of the Aztec Empire in 1521 and the fall of Tenochtitlan.

Lost treasures

After the Spanish conquered Montezuma II and Tenochtitlan, they went in search of more Aztec treasures. If people tried to stop them from taking their gold, food or other goods, they were killed. The Spanish melted down many of the treasures and artefacts. For example, the invaders seized vast quantities of gold and melted it into bars that were easier to transport back to Europe. Also, to encourage the Aztecs to give up their gods and convert to the Spanish Catholic religion, Aztec temples were demolished. Aztec libraries containing thousands of works on many subjects, which could have told us even more about their amazing civilization than we know today, were burned to the ground. However, even though the empire was gone, the Aztecs did not disappear completely: Tenochtitlan became Mexico City, and many people of Mexican descent have **ancestors** who were Aztecs.

ANSWERS

Did you manage to analyse the ancients? Check your answers against the correct answers on these pages.

PAGE 9

1. By paying tributes to the Aztec emperor, people were allowed to rule themselves.
2. The fact that these tributes include items from far away from Tenochtitlan helps us understand how far the Aztec Empire spread and how far the Aztecs ruled.

PAGE 13

1. Masks were believed to be very powerful and important so this mask is made of turquoise, which was very valuable, sacred and represented life itself.
2. The mask was designed to look scary so that people were in awe of and had respect for the powerful god Tezcatlipoca.

PAGE 19

1. The steps have stone serpent heads to ward off evil spirits.
2. The pyramid was designed to be tall so that commoners could not see the temple from the bottom. Only priests and leaders were allowed to climb the steps to the temple at the top, to be near the gods.

PAGE 25

1. Gold objects, such as labrets, were worn only by high chiefs and royalty. Labrets were worn below the lower lip to symbolize the fact that the ruler spoke for the gods.
2. The Aztecs believed that serpents could move on land, in water and among trees, just as the gods could travel across land, water and through the skies. This made serpents sacred, or holy, to the Aztecs.

ANSWERS

PAGE 33

1. The warriors wore jaguar costumes to show they were brave and successful, because the jaguar was a symbol of the power of Tezcatlipoca, the god of the night sky. They also believed the skins gave them the strength of jaguars during battles. When they led warriors into battle, their costumes also scared the enemy.
2. The jaguar warrior is holding a round shield (probably covered in feathers) and a macuahuitl, which was likely made of wood with jagged pieces of sharp obsidian along its edges.

PAGE 41

1. The fact that the god of games, Xochipilli, is shown watching the patolli players reminds us that religion was a part of every aspect of the Aztecs' daily lives, even when they were playing games. It shows they believed that praying and giving offerings to a god could bring them luck and impact everything that happened, even the throw of dice (or beans)!
2. The five symbols at the top of the picture are probably the five beans or patolli that are used as dice and from which the game of patolli gets its name.

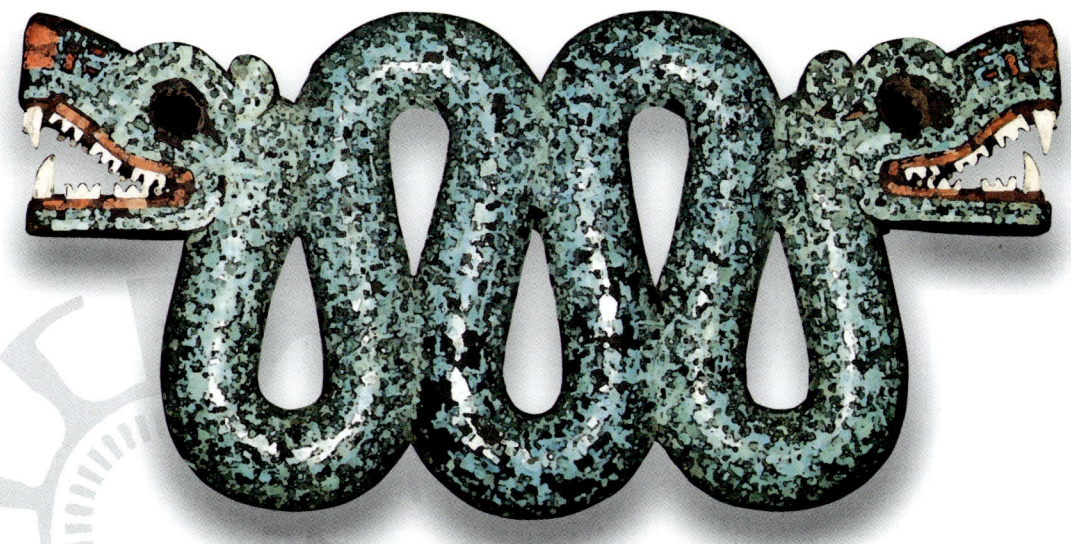

45

GLOSSARY

afterlife life after death

ancestors relatives from previous generations who have died

architects people who design and plan buildings

artefacts objects from the past that tell us about people's lives in history

bartered exchanged goods or services for other goods or services

city-state city that with its surrounding area forms an independent state

civilizations settled and stable communities in which people live together peacefully and use systems such as writing to communicate

embroidered decorated with stitches made by sewing

emperor a male ruler or king; an empress is a female ruler or queen

empire a large area of land or a group of countries ruled over by one leader

exported took or sold goods to another country

faeces waste matter or droppings

foundations solid structures that support a building from underneath

imported bought and brought goods from another country

incense a substance burned to give off a pleasant smell, often used in religious rituals

merchants people who buy and sell goods

Mesoamerica the name for the region of Mexico and Central America where the Aztecs lived

monuments statues, buildings or other structures made to remember an event, time or person

offerings things that people give as part of a religious ceremony or ritual

reservoirs artificial lakes for collecting and storing water

resin a sticky substance produced by trees

rituals ceremonies performed for religious reasons

sacrifices animals or people killed to honour a god or gods

society a large group of people living together in an organized way, often sharing a religion, making decisions about how to do things and sharing work that needs to be done

tombs buildings where dead people are put to rest

trade guilds groups of people who work together at the same trade

umbilical cord the tube that connects a baby in the womb to its mother and supplies it with nutrients

underworld the mythical world of the dead

FIND OUT MORE

Books

Aztecs (Explore!), Izzie Howell (Wayland, 2018)

The Aztec Empire (Horrors from History), Louise Spilsbury (Raintree, 2020)

The Aztec Empire (You Choose: Historical Eras), Elizabeth Raum (Raintree, 2015)

The Aztecs (At Home With), Tim Cooke (Wayland, 2017)

You Wouldn't Want to Be an Aztec Sacrifice (Revised Edition), Fiona MacDonald (Franklin Watts, 2013)

Websites

There are fun facts about the Aztecs at:
www.dkfindout.com/uk/history/aztecs

Learn more about the amazing Aztecs at:
www.history.com/topics/aztecs

There are lots of Aztec topics to choose from at:
www.historyonthenet.com/tag/aztec

INDEX

Acamapichtli 4
afterlife 14–15
archaeologists 8
artists 7, 31

ball games 41
Binding of the Years 21
board games 41
boys 36, 37
braids 29, 30

cacao beans 23, 39
calendars 11, 20–21
ceremonies 10, 11, 12, 13, 20, 21, 25, 36, 40
chewing gum (chicle) 39
chinampas 22
clothing 35
codices 9, 14, 26–27, 41
commoners 7, 19, 32, 34–35
Cortés, Hernán 42
craftspeople 24–25

dolls 37
drums 40

families 36–37
farmers 7, 22, 23, 32, 37
farming 16, 22, 23, 38
feathers 9, 11, 23, 24, 27, 29, 30, 31, 35, 42
foods 23, 38–39

girls 34, 36, 37
gods 4, 7, 10–13, 14, 15, 17, 18, 19, 20, 21, 25, 29, 33, 41
gold 23, 25, 41, 42
Great Temple of the Aztecs 18, 29

headdresses 6, 24, 29, 42
houses 34
Huitzilopochtli 4, 10, 11, 14

jaguar skins 9, 30, 33
jewellery 6, 8, 35

knives 12, 20

labrets 25
Lake Texcoco 4, 16
language (Nahuatl) 7
Lord of the Dead 15

macuahuitl 30
markets 23, 24, 35
masks 7, 13, 15
merchants (pochteca) 7, 24
Mexico City 5, 43
Mictlan 14, 15
mirrors 34
Montezuma II 5, 17, 42
mosaics 12, 13
musical instruments 40

nobles 6, 7, 15, 24, 26, 28, 34, 39, 41
number system 27

obsidian 16, 30, 34

palaces 8, 17
population 5, 16
pottery 24, 36, 39
priests 6, 7, 10, 11, 12, 13, 14, 19, 28
prisoners of war 7, 12, 30, 32, 33
pyramids 12, 16, 17, 18, 19, 20, 32

Quetzalcoatl 11, 18

reservoirs 16
rituals 13, 18, 20, 21, 24, 25, 26, 36, 40
ruins 5, 18, 19
rulers 5, 6, 17, 42

sacrifices 10, 11, 12–13, 14, 18, 20, 41
schools 37
sculptures 5, 6, 29
serfs 7
serpents 5, 8, 11, 19, 25
skulls 13, 18, 32
slaves 7, 12, 34, 35, 37
Spanish invaders 8, 42–43
Sun Stone 20, 21

taxes 6, 7, 26
temples 5, 8, 10, 11, 12, 13, 16, 18–19, 20, 24, 32, 37, 43
Tenochtitlan 4, 5, 6, 9, 10, 11, 16, 17, 18, 23, 24, 29, 42, 43
Tezcatlipoca 13, 33
Tlaloc 11
tombs 8
tributes 9, 26, 27, 42
turquoise 13

umbilical cords 36
underworld 14, 15, 19

warriors 5, 14, 28–29, 30–31, 32–33, 36, 40, 41
water 16, 22, 25, 34
weapons 8, 30–31, 42
women 34, 35